Quotes
to
Write
By

QUOTES
TO
WRITE
BY

Daily Inspiration and
Guidance for Writers

Kristy Taylor

KT PUBLISHING
www.ktp.com.au

Published by
KT Publishing
PO Box 584
Caboolture Qld 4510
AUSTRALIA
www.ktp.com.au

National Library of Australia Cataloguing-in-Publication Data:
Taylor, Kristy.
Quotes to write by: daily inspiration and guidance for writers.
ISBN 0 9752298 2 6.
1. Authorship. 2. Writing – Quotations, maxims, etc. I. Title.
808.02

Welcome

The act of writing makes easier the actual writing. Sitting down at your desk with pen in hand, or fingers on keyboard, will greatly increase your chances of getting started for the day. But if your muse has left you or motivation is lacking, reach for your copy of Quotes to Write By. A complete year of quotes, one for each day, will help get your creative juices flowing. Be guided and inspired by fellow writers and celebrities from around the globe.

Open to today's date for an inspirational or guiding quote to help get your writing back on schedule. Quotes to Write By is a helpful resource of encouragement for every writer.

Kristy Taylor
www.kristytaylor.com

Visit www.writingaustralia.com for a free newsletter and membership website jam packed with information for writers: markets, publishers, articles, competitions, ebooks, software, writer's pages, agents, message board, bookshelf and our showcase of fiction, poetry and essays submitted (contracted) by writers from around the world.

1st January

"One hasn't become a writer until one has distilled writing into a habit, and that habit has been forced into an obsession. Writing has to be an obsession. It has to be something as organic, physiological and psychological as speaking or sleeping or eating."

Niyi Osundare

2nd January

"The art of writing is the art of applying the seat of the pants to the seat of the chair."

Mary Heaton Vorse

3rd January

"Use what talent you possess:
the woods would be very silent if no birds sang
except those that sang best."

Henry Van Dyke

4th January

"If the writer has a masterpiece within, he had better save it on paper. Otherwise, none of us will ever miss it."

Steve Martini

5th January

"Good work doesn't happen with inspiration. It comes with constant, often tedious and deliberate effort. If your vision of a writer involves sitting in a cafe, sipping an aperitif with one's fellow geniuses, become a drunk. It's easier and far less exhausting."

William Hefferman

6th January

"It's always too early to quit."

Norman Vincent Peale

7th January

""You need a certain amount of
nerve to be a writer."

Margaret Atwood

8th January

"Success seems to be largely a matter of hanging on after others have let go."

William Feather

9th January

"Writing energy is like anything else: The more you put in, the more you get out."

Richard Reeves

10th January

"Keep away from people who try to belittle your ambitions. Small people always do that, but the really great make you feel that you, too, can become great."

Mark Twain

11ᵗʰ January

"Far away in the sunshine are my highest inspirations. I may not reach them, but I can look up and see the beauty, believe in them and try to follow where they may lead."

Lousia May Alcott

12th January

"Success comes before work only
in the dictionary."

Anonymous

13th January

"Don't sell yourself short; dare to dream. You might sell to a top market before you ever sell to a non-paying market - you won't know unless you try. In the same way, it's good to be cooperative, but don't be too humble either."

Rheal Nadeau

14th January

"Experience is one thing you can't
get for nothing."

Oscar Wilde

15th January

"When I start a book, I always think it's patently absurd that I can write one. No one, certainly not me, can write a book 500 pages long. But I know I can write 15 pages, and if I write 15 pages every day, eventually I will have 500 of them."

John Saul

16th January

"Hold fast to dreams, for if dreams die, life is a broken bird that cannot fly."

Langston Hughes

17th January

"Writing a novel is like driving a car at night.
You can see only as far as your headlights, but
you can make the whole trip that way."

E.L. Doctorow

18th January

"Even if you are on the right track, you'll get run over if you just sit there."

Will Rogers

19th January

"If you can imagine it,
You can achieve it.
If you can dream it,
You can become it."

William Arthur Ward

20th January

"Don't say you don't have enough time. You have exactly the same number of hours per day that were given to Helen Keller, Pasteur, Michelangelo, Mother Teresa, Leonardo da Vinci, Thomas Jefferson, and Albert Einstein."

H. Jackson Brown

21st January

"Good writing is supposed to evoke sensation in the reader - not the fact that it is raining, but the feeling of being rained upon."

E.L. Doctorow

22nd January

"A ratio of failures is built into the process of writing. The wastebasket has evolved for a reason."

Margaret Atwood

23rd January

"What I adore is supreme professionalism. I'm bored by writers who can write only when it's raining."

Noel Coward

24th January

"The worst thing you write is better than the best thing you didn't write."

Unknown

25th January

"This manuscript of yours that has just come back from another editor is a precious package. Don't consider it rejected. Consider that you've addressed it 'to the editor who can appreciate my work' and it has simply come back stamped 'Not at this address'. Just keep looking for the right address."

Barbara Kingsolver

26th January

"He is able who thinks he is able."

Buddha

27th January

"By making writing a part of your daily routine, just like brushing your teeth, you'll discipline yourself to work as a writer instead of a hobbyist who only writes when there's some fun to be had."

Theresa Grant

28ᵗʰ January

"Nothing great in the world has ever been accomplished without passion."

G.W.F. Hegel

29th January

"My great concern is not whether you have failed, but whether you are content with your failure."

Abraham Lincoln

30th January

"Becoming the reader is the essence of becoming a writer."

John O'Hara

31st January

"You may be disappointed if you fail, but you are doomed if you don't try."

Beverly Sills

1st February

"What I had to face, the very bitter lesson that
everyone who wants to write has got to learn,
was that a thing may in itself be the finest piece
of writing one has ever done, and yet have
absolutely no place in the manuscript one
hopes to publish."

Thomas Wolfe

2nd February

"That which we persist in doing becomes easier - not that the nature of the task has changed, but our ability to do has increased."

Emerson

3rd February

"Making the simple complicated is commonplace; making the complicated simple, awesomely simple, that's creativity."

Charles Mingus

4th February

"When I sit at my table to write, I never know what it's going to be until I'm under way. I trust in inspiration, which sometimes comes and sometimes doesn't. But I don't sit back waiting for it. I work every day."

Alberto Moravia

5th February

"If you would not be forgotten, as soon as you are dead and rotten, either write things worth reading, or do things worth the writing."

Benjamin Franklin

6th February

"Our doubts are traitors,
And make us lose the good we oft might win
By fearing to attempt."

William Shakespeare

7th February

"It takes most of us a long time to learn our craft. So keep at it. Don't give up."

Jacqueline Briskin

8th February

"I think the only person a writer has an obligation to is himself. If what I write doesn't fulfill something in me, if I don't honestly feel it's the best I can do, then I'm miserable."

Truman Capote

9th February

"If you would be a writer, first be a reader. Only through the assimilation of ideas, thoughts and philosophies can one begin to focus his own ideas, thoughts and philosophies."

Allan W. Eckert

10th February

"Don't let life discourage you; everyone who got where he is had to begin where he was."

Richard L. Evans

11th February

"I have never thought of myself as a good writer. Anyone who wants reassurance of that should read one of my first drafts. But I'm one of the world's great rewriters."

James A. Michener

12th February

"No one put a gun to your head and ordered you to become a writer. One writes out of his own choice and must be prepared to take the rough spots along the road with a certain equanimity, though allowed some grinding of the teeth."

Stanley Ellin

13th February

"The hard part is getting to the top of page 1."

Tom Stoppard

14th February

"It is perfectly okay to write garbage - as long as you edit brilliantly."

C.J. Cherryh

15th February

"I have seldom written a story, long or short, that I did not have to write and rewrite. There are single stories of mine that have taken me ten or twelve years to get written."

Sherwood Anderson

16th February

"A great deal of talent is lost to the world for want of a little courage. Every day sends to their graves obscure men whose timidity prevented them from making a first effort."

Sydney Smith

17th February

"Start early and work hard. A writer's apprenticeship usually involves writing a million words (which are then discarded) before he's almost ready to begin. That takes a while."

David Eddings

18th February

"Writing is like hunting. There are brutally cold afternoons with nothing in sight, only the wind and your breaking heart. Then the moment when you bag something big. The entire process is beyond intoxicating."

Kate Braverman

19th February

"Nothing is particularly hard if you divide it into small jobs."

Henry Ford

20th February

"Writing is rewriting. A writer must learn to deepen characters, trim writing, intensify scenes. To fall in love with a first draft to the point where one cannot change it is to greatly enhance the prospects of never publishing."

Richard North Patterson

21st February

"Wake the happy words."

Theodore Roethke

22nd February

"Dreaming and hoping won't produce a piece of work; only writing, rewriting and rewriting (if necessary) - a devoted translation of thoughts and dreams into words on paper - will result in a story."

Roberta Gellis

23rd February

"Write what you care about and understand. Writers should never try to outguess the marketplace in search of a saleable idea; the simple truth is that all good books will eventually find a publisher if the writer tries hard enough, and a central secret to writing a good book is to write one that people like you will enjoy."

Richard North Patterson

24th February

"Books aren't written - they're rewritten.
Including your own. It is one of the hardest
things to accept, especially after the seventh
rewrite hasn't quite done it."

Michael Crichton

25th February

"There is no perfect time to write.
There's only now."

Barbara Kingsolver

26th February

"I turn sentences around. That's my life. I write a sentence and then I turn it around. Then I look at it and I turn it around again. Then I have lunch. Then I come back in and write another sentence. Then I have tea and turn the new sentence around. Then I read the two sentences over and turn them both around. Then I lie down on my sofa and think. Then I get up and throw them out and start from the beginning."

Raymond Carver

27th February

"In composing, as a general rule, run a pen through every other word you have written; you have no idea what vigor it will give your style."

Sydney Smith

28th February

"I write as straight as I can, just as I walk as straight as I can, because that is the best way to get there."

H.G. Wells

1st March

"The task of a writer consists of being able to make something out of an idea."

Thomas Mann

2nd March

"The difference between the right word and the almost right word is the difference between lightning and the lightning bug."

Mark Twain

3rd March

"I have written a great many stories and I still don't know how to go about it except to write it and take my chances."

John Steinbeck

4th March

"Writing is not a profession, occupation or job; it is not a way of life: it is a comprehensive response to life."

Gregory McDonald

5th March

"The difference between reality and fiction?
Fiction has to make sense."

Tom Clancy

6th March

"Writing well is the best revenge."

Dorothy Parker

7th **March**

"I don't think it's very useful to open wide the door for young artists; the ones who break down the door are more interesting."

Paul Schrader

8th March

"Put it before them briefly so they will read it, clearly so they will appreciate it, picturesquely so they will remember it and, above all, accurately so they will be guided by its light."

Joseph Pulitzer

9th March

"Writing is easy: All you do is sit staring at a blank sheet of paper until drops of blood form on your forehead."

Gene Fowler

10th March

"If a book is not alive in the writer's mind, it is
as dead as year-old horse-shit."

Stephen King

11th March

"When I was a young boy, they called me a liar.
Now that I'm all grown up, they call me a writer."

Isaac Bashevis Singer

12th March

"In your writing, be strong, defiant, forbearing. Have a point to make and write to it. Dare to say what you want most to say, and say it as plainly as you can. Whether or not you write well, write bravely."

Bill Stout

13ᵗʰ March

"I write for the same reason I breathe - because
if I didn't, I would die."

Isaac Asimov

14th March

"If there is a gun hanging on the wall in the first act, it must fire in the last."

Anton Chekhov

15th March

"However great a man's natural talent may be, the act of writing cannot be learned all at once."

Jean Jacques Rousseau

16th March

"Just get it down on paper, and then we'll see
what to do about it."

Maxwell Perkins

17th March

"There is no rule on how to write. Sometimes it comes easily and perfectly: sometimes it's like drilling rock and then blasting it out with charges."

Ernest Hemingway

18th March

"When I face the desolate impossibility of writing five hundred pages a sick sense of failure falls on me and I know I can never do it. This happens every time. Then gradually I write one page and then another. One day's work is all I can permit myself to contemplate and I eliminate the possibility of ever finishing."

John Steinbeck

19th March

"No tears in the writer, no tears in the reader.
No surprise in the writer, no surprise in
the reader."

Robert Frost

20th March

"It is not the critic who counts, not the man who points out how the strong man stumbled, or where the doer of deeds could have done them better. The credit belongs to the man who is actually in the arena; whose face is marred by dust and sweat and blood; who strives valiantly; who errs and comes short again and again; who knows the great enthusiasms; the great devotions; and spends himself in a worthy cause; who, at the best, knows in the end the triumph of high achievement and at the worst, if he fails, at least fails while daring greatly, so that his place shall never be with those cold and timid souls who know neither victory nor defeat."

Theodore Roosevelt

21st March

"Get your facts first, and then you can distort them as much as you please."

Mark Twain

22nd March

"No, it's not a very good story - its author was
too busy listening to other voices to listen as
closely as he should have to the one coming
from inside."

Stephen King

23rd March

"Find a subject you care about and which you in your heart feel others should care about. It is this genuine caring, not your games with language, which will be the most compelling and seductive element in your style."

Kurt Vonnegut

24th March

"We are what we repeatedly do. Excellence, then, is not an act, but a habit."

Aristotle

25th **March**

"It is a cheap trick merely to surprise and shock the reader, especially at the expense of logic. And a lack of invention on the writers' part cannot be covered up by sensational action and clever prose. It is also a kind of laziness to write the obvious, which does not entertain, really. The idea is an unexpected turn of events, reasonably consistent with the characters of the protagonists. Stretch the reader's credulity, his sense of logic, to the utmost - it is quite elastic - but don't break it. In this way, you will write something new, surprising and entertaining both to yourself and the reader."

Patricia Highsmith

26th March

"You must want to enough. Enough to take all the rejections, enough to pay the price of disappointment and discouragement while you are learning. Like any other artist you must learn your craft - then you can add all the genius you like."

Phyllis A. Whitney

27th March

"The first chapter sells the book;
the last chapter sells the next book."

Mickey Spillane

28th March

"A writer is someone for whom writing is more difficult than it is for other people."

Thomas Mann

29th March

"Often I'll find clues to where the story might go
by figuring out where the characters would
rather not go."

Doug Lawson

30th March

"There are three rules for writing a novel.
Unfortunately, no one knows what they are."

W. Somerset Maugham

31st March

"Omit needless words.
Vigorous writing is concise. A sentence should
contain no unnecessary words, a paragraph no
unnecessary sentences, for the same reason that
a drawing should have no unnecessary lines and
a machine no unnecessary parts."

William Strunk, Jr.

1st April

"The mere habit of writing, of constantly keeping at it, of never giving up, ultimately teaches you how to write."

Gabriel Fielding

2nd April

"Writing is like cooking... if you spill something, you should make it look like part of the act."

John Keeble

3rd April

"Writing is easy. You just sit down at the
typewriter and open a vein."

Red Smith

4th April

"I notice that you use plain, simple language, short words and brief sentences. That is the way to write English - it is the modern way and the best way. Stick to it; don't let fluff and flowers and verbosity creep in. When you catch an adjective, kill it. No, I don't mean utterly, but kill most of them - then the rest will be valuable. They weaken when they are close together. They give strength when they are wide apart. An adjective habit, or a wordy, diffuse, flowery habit, once fastened upon a person, is as hard to get rid of as any other vice."

Mark Twain

5th April

"Writing is a lot like sex. At first you do it because you like it. Then you find yourself doing it for a few close friends and people you like. But if you're any good at all... you end up doing it for money."

Unknown

6th April

"I have tried simply to write the best I can. Sometimes I have good luck and write better than I can."

Ernest Hemingway

7th April

"Being a writer is like having homework every
night for the rest of your life."

Lawrence Kasdan

8th April

"We are cups, constantly and quietly being filled. The trick is, knowing how to tip ourselves over and let the beautiful stuff out."

Ray Bradbury

9th April

"What is written without effort is in general read
without pleasure."

Samuel Johnson

10th April

"Manuscript: something submitted in haste and returned at leisure."

Oliver Herford

11th April

"The profession of book-writing makes horse racing seem like a solid, stable business."

John Steinbeck

12th April

"You can't say 'I won't write today' because that excuse will extend into several days, then several months, then... you are not a writer anymore, just someone who dreams about being a writer."

Dorothy C. Fontana

13th April

"Never write anything that does not give you great pleasure. Emotion is easily transferred from the writer to the reader."

Joseph Joubert

14th April

"A successful book is not made of what is in it,
but what is left out of it."

Mark Twain

15th April

"What no wife of a writer can ever understand is that a writer is working when he's staring out the window."

Rudolph Erich Rascoe

16th April

"For anyone who is: just keep writing. Keep reading. If you are meant to be a writer, a storyteller, it'll work itself out. You just keep feeding it your energy, and giving it that crucial chance to work itself out. By reading and writing."

Robin McKinley

17th April

"I cannot start a story or chapter without knowing how it ends. Of course, it rarely ends that way."

Kashua Ishigura

18th April

"A profound theme is of trifling importance if the characters knocked around by it are uninteresting, and brilliant technique is a nuisance if it pointlessly prevents us from seeing the characters and what they do."

John Gardner

19th April

"People want to know why I do this, why I write such gross stuff. I like to tell them that I have the heart of a small boy - and I keep it in a jar on my desk."

Stephen King

20th April

"I always stopped when I knew what was going to happen next. That way I could be sure of going on the next day."

Ernest Hemingway

21st April

"You can take for granted that people know more or less what a street, a shop, a beach, a sky, an oak tree looks like. Tell them what makes this one different."

Neil Gaiman

22nd April

"The cure for writer's cramp is writer's block."

Inigo de Leon

23rd April

"No one can write a best seller by trying to. He must write with complete sincerity; the clichés that make you laugh, the hackneyed characters, the well-worn situations, the commonplace story that excites your derision, seem neither hackneyed, well worn nor commonplace to him. The conclusion is obvious: you cannot write anything that will convince unless you are yourself convinced. The best seller sells because he writes with his heart's blood."

Somerset Maugham

24th April

"Don't mistake a good setup for a satisfying
conclusion - many beginning writers end their
stories when the real story is just ready
to begin."

Stanley Schmidt

25th April

"After all, most writing is done away from the typewriter, away from the desk. I'd say it occurs in the quiet, silent moments, while you're walking or shaving or playing a game, or whatever, or even talking to someone you're not vitally interested in."

Henry Miller

26th April

"What is easy to read has been difficult to write.
The labour of writing and rewriting, correcting
and recorrecting, is the due exacted by every
good book from its author, even if he knows
from the beginning exactly what he wants to say.
A limpid style is invariably the result of hard
labour, and the easily flowing connection of
sentence with sentence and paragraph with
paragraph has always been won by the sweat
of the brow."

G. M. Trevelyan

27th April

"All writers are vain, selfish and lazy, and at the very bottom of their motives lies a mystery. Writing a book is a long, exhausting struggle, like a long bout of some painful illness. One would never undertake such a thing if one were not driven by some demon whom one can neither resist nor understand."

George Orwell

28th April

"Read over your compositions, and where ever you meet with a passage which you think is particularly fine, strike it out."

Samuel Johnson

29th April

"Good writers may 'tell' about almost anything in fiction except the characters' feelings. One may tell the reader that the character went to a private school (one need not show a scene at the private school if the scene has no importance for the rest of the narrative), or one may tell the reader that the character hates spaghetti; but with rare exceptions the characters' feelings must be demonstrated: fear, love, excitement, doubt, embarrassment, despair become real only when they take the form of events - action (or gesture), dialogue, or physical reaction to setting. Detail is the lifeblood of fiction."

John Gardner

30th April

"The time to begin writing an article is when you have finished it to your satisfaction. By that time you begin to clearly and logically perceive what it is that you really want to say."

Mark Twain

1ˢᵗ May

"If you're going to write, don't pretend to write down. It's going to be the best you can do, and it's the fact that it's the best you can do that kills you."

Dorothy Parker

2nd May

"Mere literary talent is common; what is rare is endurance, the continuing desire to work hard at writing."

Donald Hall

3rd May

"There is no Idea Dump, no Story Central, no Island of Buried Bestsellers; good story ideas seem to come quite literally from nowhere, sailing at you right out of the empty sky: two previously unrelated ideas come together and make something new under the sun. Your job isn't to find these ideas but to recognize them when they show up."

Stephen King

4th May

"I perceived that to express those impressions, to write that essential book, which is the only true one, a great writer does not, in the current meaning of the word, invent it, but, since it exists already in each one of us, interprets it. The duty and the task of a writer are those of an interpreter."

Marcel Proust

5th May

"Every morning between 9.00 and 12.00
I go to my room and sit before a piece of paper.
Many times, I just sit for three hours with no
ideas coming to me. But I know one thing. If an
idea does come between 9.00 and 12.00
I am there ready for it."

Flannery O'Connor

6th May

"As with all other aspects of the narrative art, you will improve with practice, but practice will never make you perfect. Why should it? What fun would that be?"

Stephen King

7th May

"A good novel tells us the truth about its hero;
but a bad novel tells us the truth about
its author."

G.K. Chesterton

8th May

"To write something, you have to risk making a
fool of yourself."

Anne Rice

9th May

"James Blish told me I had the worst case of 'said bookism' (that is, using every word except said to indicate dialogue). He told me to limit the verbs to said, replied, asked, and answered and only when absolutely necessary."

Anne MacCaffrey

10th May

"The complete novelist would come into the world with a catalog of qualities like this. He would own the concentration of a Trappist monk, the organizational ability of a Prussian field marshal, the insight into human relations of a Viennese psychologist, the discipline of a man who prints the Lord's Prayer on the head of a pin, the exquisite sense of timing of an Olympic gymnast, and by the way, a natural instinct and flair for exceptional use of language."

Leon Uris

11th May

"Books choose their authors; the act of creation
is not entirely a rational and conscious one."

Salman Rushdie

12th May

"I'm writing a book.
I've got the page numbers done."

Steven Wright

13th May

"Three Rules for Literary Success:
1. Read a lot.
2. Write a lot.
3. Read a lot more, write a lot more."

Robert Silverberg

14th May

"In going where you have to go, and doing what you have to do, and seeing what you have to see, you dull and blunt the instrument you write with. But I would rather have it bent and dulled and know I had to put it on the grindstone again and hammer it into shape and put a whetstone to it, and know that I had something to write about, than to have it bright and shining and nothing to say, or smooth and well oiled in the closet, but unused."

Ernest Hemingway

15th May

"I am paid by the word, so I always write the shortest words possible."

Bertrand Russell

16th May

"The art of fiction does not begin until the
novelist thinks of his story as a matter to be
shown, to be so exhibited that it will tell itself."

Percy Lubbock

17th May

"Short stories are designed to deliver their impact in as few pages as possible. A tremendous amount is left out, and a good short story writer learns to include only the most essential information."

Orson Scott Card

18th May

"When an author is too meticulous about his style, you may presume that his mind is frivolous and his content flimsy."

Seneca

19th May

"At the beginning of their careers many writers have a need to overwrite. They choose carefully turned-out phrases; they want to impress their readers with their large vocabularies. By the excesses of their language, these young men and women try to hide their sense of inexperience. With maturity the writer becomes more secure in his ideas. He finds his real tone and develops a simple and effective style."

Jorge Luis Borges

20th May

"All fiction is a process of imagining: whatever you write, in whatever genre or medium, your task is to make things up convincingly and interestingly and new."

Neil Gaiman

21st May

"Thus, with child to speak, and helpless in my throes, biting my truant pen, beating myself for spite: Fool! said my muse to me, look in thy heart, and write."

Sir Philip Sidney

22nd May

"Obscenities are too often used for shock value, as a kind of shorthand for real expression of emotion. You've got to scale down your monstrosities. A scream is not a discovery."

John L'Heureux

23rd May

"You need more than a beginning if you're going to start a book. If all you have is a beginning, then once you've written that beginning, you have nowhere to go."

Neil Gaiman

24th May

"The best way to become acquainted with a subject is to write a book about it."

Benjamin Disraeli

25th May

"Suit the action to the word,
the word to the action."

William Shakespeare

26th May

"Sometimes you have to go on when you don't feel like it, and sometimes you're doing good work when it feels like all you're managing is to shovel shit from a sitting position."

Stephen King

27th May

"What I like in a good author isn't what he says,
but what he whispers."

Logan Pearsall Smith

28th May

"You must keep sending work out; you must never let a manuscript do nothing but eat its head off in a drawer. You send that work out again and again, while you're working on another one. If you have talent, you will receive some measure of success - but only if you persist."

Isaac Asimov

29th May

"Writing a first draft is like groping one's way
into a dark room, or overhearing a faint
conversation, or telling a joke whose punch line
you've forgotten. As someone said, one writes
mainly to rewrite, for rewriting and revising are
how one's mind comes to inhabit the
material fully."

Ted Solotaroff

30th May

"You can approach the act of writing with nervousness, excitement, hopefulness, or even despair - the sense that you can never completely put on the page what's in your mind and heart. You can come to the act with your fists clenched and your eyes narrowed, ready to kick ass and take down names. You can come to it because you want a girl to marry you or because you want to change the world. Come to it any way but lightly. Let me say it again: you must not come lightly to the blank page."

Stephen King

31st May

"Agatha Christie has given more pleasure in bed than any other woman."

Nancy Banks Smith

1st June

"We have to continually be jumping off cliffs and developing our wings on the way down."

Kurt Vonnegut

2nd June

"It is better to write a bad first draft than to write no first draft at all."

Will Shetterly

3rd June

"The writer does the most good who gives his reader the most knowledge and takes from him the least time."

Sydney Smith

4th June

"Say all you have to say in the fewest possible words, or your reader will be sure to skip them; and in the plainest possible words or he will certainly misunderstand them."

John Ruskin

5th June

"Close the door. Write with *no one* looking over your shoulder. Don't try to figure out what other people want to hear from you; figure out what you have to say. It's the one and only thing you have to offer."

Barbara Kingsolver

6th June

"It's hard for me to believe that people who read very little (or not at all in some cases) should presume to write and expect people to like what they have written... Can I be blunt on this subject? If you don't have time to read, you don't have the time (or the tools) to write. Simple as that."

Stephen King

7th June

"The two most engaging powers of a good author are to make new things familiar and familiar things new."

William M. Thackeray

8th June

"Inspiration is wonderful when it happens, but the writer must develop an approach for the rest of the time... The wait is simply too long."

Leonard Bernstein

9th June

"In a given scene I may know nothing more than how it's supposed to end, most of the time not even that. Scenes are improvised. A character does or says something, and with as much spontaneity and schizophrenia as I can muster, another character responds. In this way, everything I write is a spontaneous chain reaction and I'm running around playing leapfrog in my brain trying to "be" all my people."

Richard Price

10th June

"Write what you want to read. The person you know best in this world is you. Listen to yourself. If you are excited by what you are writing, you have a much better chance of putting that excitement over to a reader."

Robin McKinley

11th June

"You can never correct your work well until you have forgotten it."

Voltaire

12th June

"I was working on the proof of one of my poems all morning, and took out a comma. In the afternoon I put it back again."

Oscar Wilde

13th June

"Try and write straight English; never using
slang except in dialogue and then only when
unavoidable. Because all slang goes sour in a
short time. I only use swear words, for example,
that have lasted at least a thousand years for
fear of getting stuff that will be simply timely
and then go sour."

Ernest Hemingway

14th June

"In the final analysis, real suspense comes with moral dilemma and the courage to make and act upon choices. False suspense comes from the accidental and meaningless occurrence of one damned thing after another."

John Gardner

15th June

"I love being a writer,
what I can't stand is the paperwork."

Peter De Vries

16th June

There is only one way to defeat the enemy, and that is to write as well as one can. The best argument is an undeniably good book.

Saul Bellow

17th June

"The universe is made of stories, not of atoms."

Muriel Rukeyser

18th June

"A book worth reading only in childhood is not worth reading even then."

C.S. Lewis

19th June

"Writing is not like painting where you add. It is not what you put on the canvas that the reader sees. Writing is more like a sculpture where you remove, you eliminate in order to make the work visible. Even those pages you remove somehow remain."

Elie Wiesel

20th June

"Wear the old coat and buy the new book."

Austin Phelps

21st June

"Dialogue in fiction is what characters
do to one another."

Elizabeth Bowen

22nd June

"Without knowing the force of words, it is impossible to know men."

Confucius

23rd June

"We are nauseated by the sight of trivial
personalities decomposing in the
eternity of print."

Virginia Woolf

24th June

"From the moment I picked up your book until I laid it down, I was convulsed with laughter. Some day I intend reading it."

Groucho Marx

25th June

"The great majority of modern third-person narration is 'I' narration very thinly disguised."

John Fowles

26th June

"A word is not a crystal, transparent and unchanged, it is the skin of a living thought and may vary greatly in color and content according to the circumstances and the time in which it is used."

Oliver Wendell Holmes

27th June

"Every secret of a writer's soul, every experience of his life, every quality of his mind is written large in his works."

Virginia Woolf

28th June

"Creativity is a drug I cannot live without."

Cecil B. DeMille

29th June

"The object of the novelist is to keep the reader entirely oblivious of the fact that the author exists - even of the fact he is reading a book."

Ford Madox Ford

30th June

"It is with words as with sunbeams - the more
they are condensed, the deeper they burn."

Robert Southey

1st July

"Four basic premises of writing:
clarity, brevity, simplicity, and humanity."

William Zinsser

2nd July

"The most potent muse of all is our
own inner child."

Stephen Nachmanovitch

3rd July

"You write about the thing that sank its teeth
into you and wouldn't let go."

Paul West

4th July

"Consider the postage stamp:
its usefulness consists in the ability to
stick to one thing till it gets there."

Josh Billings

5th July

"You can't wait for inspiration.
You have to go after it with a club."

Gloria Steinem

6th July

"Cross out as many adjectives and adverbs as you can. It is comprehensible when I write: 'The man sat on the grass,' because it is clear and does not detain one's attention. On the other hand, it is difficult to figure out and hard on the brain if I write: 'The tall, narrow-chested man of medium height and with a red beard sat down on the green grass that had already been trampled down by the pedestrians, sat down silently, looking around timidly and fearfully.' The brain can't grasp all that at once, and art must be grasped at once, instantaneously."

Anton Chekhov

7th July

"They are able because they think they are able."

Vergil

8th July

"One ought to write only when one leaves a piece of one's flesh in the inkpot each time one dips one's pen."

Noel Coward

9th July

"My attitude toward punctuation is that it ought to be as conventional as possible. The game of golf would lose a good deal if croquet mallets and billiard cues were allowed on the putting green. You ought to be able to show that you can do it a good deal better than anyone else with the regular tools before you have a license to bring in your own improvements."

Ernest Hemingway

10th July

"There is no failure except in no longer trying. There is no defeat except from within, no really insurmountable barrier save our own inherent weakness of purpose."

Kin Hubbard

11th July

"I think a little menace is fine to have in a story. For one thing, it's good for the circulation."

Joseph Conrad

12th July

"The prose as such has to be singing the song the story is telling."

Leonard Michaels

13th July

"The difference between perseverance and obstinacy is, that one often comes from a strong will, and the other from a strong won't."

Henry Ward Beecher

14th July

"I like density, not volume. I like to leave something to the imagination. The reader must fit the pieces together, with the author's discreet help."

Angela Cartwright

15th July

"Simplify.
Then complicate all over again."

Paul West

16th July

"Big shots are only little shots
who keep shooting."

Christopher Morley

17th July

"Not all writers are artists. But all of us like the idea of somebody in the year 2283 blowing the dust off one of our books, thumbing through it and exclaiming, 'Hey, listen to what this old guy had to say back in the twentieth century!'"

Flannery O'Connor

18th July

"Any writer, I suppose, feels that the world into which he was born is nothing less than a conspiracy against the cultivation of his talent."

James Baldwin

19th July

"It is my ambition to say in ten sentences;
what others say in a whole book."

Nietzsche

20th July

"I used to be adjective happy. Now I cut them
with so much severity that I find I have to put a
few adjectives back."

Catherine O'Hara

21st July

"The job of the critic is
to report to us his moods."

Oscar Wilde

22nd July

"English usage is sometimes more than mere taste, judgment and education - sometimes it's sheer luck, like getting across the street."

E.B. White

23rd July

"There is only one trait that marks the writer. He is always watching. It's a kind of trick of the mind and he is born with it."

Morley Callaghan

24th July

"Nothing stinks like a pile of
unpublished writing."

Sylvia Plath

25th July

"If my doctor told me I had only six months to live, I wouldn't brood. I'd type a little faster."

Isaac Asimov

26th July

"The more articulate one is,
the more dangerous words become."

Maureen Howard

27th July

"The free-lance writer is a man who is paid per piece or per word or perhaps."

Robert Benchley

28th July

"Arguments over grammar and style are often as fierce as those over IBM versus Mac, and as fruitless as Coke versus Pepsi and boxers versus briefs."

Jack Lynch

29th July

"Half my life is an act of revision."

Christopher Morley

30th July

"When I want to read a novel, I write one."

Benjamin Disraeli

31st July

"Writing is a solitary occupation. Family, friends, and society are the natural enemies of the writer. He must be alone, uninterrupted, and slightly savage if he is to sustain and complete an undertaking."

Jessamyn West

1st August

"Fortunately both my wife and my mother-in-law seem to love digging up mistakes in spelling, punctuation, etc... I can hear them in the next room laughing at me."

John Irving

2nd August

"When I get a little money I buy books;
and if any is left I buy food and clothes."

Erasmus

3rd August

"There are some books that refuse to be written. They stand their ground year after year and will not be persuaded. It isn't because the book is not there and worth being written - it is only because the right form of the story does not present itself. There is only one right form for a story and if you fail to find that form the story will not tell itself."

Mark Twain

4th August

"There is also the minority of gifted, willful people who are determined to live their own lives to the end, and writers belong in this class."

Wystan Hugh Auden

5th August

"We never tire of the friendships
we form with books."

Charles Dickens

6th August

"Anybody can make history.
Only a great man can write it."

Oscar Wilde

7th August

"You always feel when you look it straight in the eye that you could have put more into it, could have let yourself go and dug harder."

George Orwell

8th August

"A big leather-bound volume makes an ideal razor strap. A thin book is useful to stick under a table with a broken caster to steady it. A large, flat atlas can be used to cover a window with a broken pane. And a thick, old-fashioned heavy book with a clasp is the finest thing in the world to throw at a noisy cat."

Mark Twain

9th August

"I don't wait for moods. You accomplish nothing if you do that. Your mind must know it has got to get down to work."

Pearl S. Buck

10th August

"To be occasionally quoted is the
only fame I hope for."

Alice Walker

11th August

"The secret is to start a story near the ending."

Chris Offut

12th August

"In a mood of faith and hope my work goes on.
A ream of fresh paper lies on my desk waiting for
the next book. I am a writer and I take up my
pen to write."

Pearl S. Buck

13th August

"Writing has made me rich - not in money but in a couple hundred characters out there, whose pursuits and anguish and triumphs I've shared. I am unspeakably grateful at the life I have come to lead."

Andrew Holleran

14th August

"We slip into a dream, forgetting the room we're sitting in, forgetting it's lunchtime or time to go to work. We recreate, with minor and for the most part unimportant changes, the vivid and continuous dream the writer worked out in his mind (revising and revising until he got it right) and captured in language so that other human beings, whenever they feel like it, may open his book and dream that dream again."

John Gardner

15th August

"It is worth mentioning, for future reference, that the creative power which bubbles so pleasantly in beginning a new book quiets down after a time, and one goes on more steadily. Doubts creep in. Then one becomes resigned. Determination not to give in, and the sense of an impending shape keep one at it more than anything."

Virginia Woolf

16th August

"Always grab the reader by the throat in the first paragraph, sink your thumbs into his windpipe in the second, and hold him against the wall until the tag line."

Wright Morris

17th August

"I don't take drugs, I take books."

Ingeborg Bachmann

18th August

"Fill your paper with the breathings of your heart..."

William Wordsworth

19th August

"I never know quite when a book starts. I don't worry about it too much. I don't believe in forcing the pace. I take it when I can, sort of seize the moment."

Le Anne Schreiber

20th August

"If you write well,
you don't have to dress funny."

James Dickey

21st August

"If I could read a book,
I'd definitely read one of yours."

Paris Hilton

22nd August

"I rather fancy most authors think of a character and then think of what he would do, while I think of something to be done and then think of the most interesting character to do it."

Edgar Allen Poe

23rd August

"A writer's inspiration is not just to create.
He must eat three times a day."

Pierre Beaumarchais

24th August

"Every great and original writer, in proportion as he is great and original, must himself create the taste by which he is to be relished."

William Wordsworth

25th August

"To me the greatest pleasure of writing is not what it's about, but the music the words make."

Truman Capote

26th August

"Being a real writer means being able to do the work on a bad day."

Norman Mailer

27th August

"It's a delicious thing to write. To be no longer
yourself but to move in an entire universe of
your own creating."

Gustave Flaubert

28th August

"Imagination is more important than knowledge.
Knowledge is limited. Imagination encircles
the world."

Albert Einstein

29th August

"Successful writers are not the ones who write the best sentences. They are the ones who keep writing. They are the ones who discover what is most important and strangest and most pleasurable in themselves, and keep believing in the value of their work, despite the difficulties."

Bonnie Friedman

30th August

"Writing a book is an adventure. To begin with,
it is a toy and an amusement. Then it becomes a
mistress, then it becomes a master, then it
becomes a tyrant. The last phase is that just as
you are about to be reconciled to your servitude,
you kill the monster, and fling him
to the public."

Winston Churchill

31st August

"A professional writer is an amateur
who didn't quit."

Richard Bach

1st September

"Writing is the only profession where no one considers you ridiculous if you earn no money."

Jules Renard

2nd September

"One of my standard, and fairly true, responses to the question as to how story ideas come to me is that story ideas only come to me for short stories. With longer fiction, it is a character (or characters) coming to visit, and I am then obliged to collaborate with him/her/it/them in creating the story."

Roger Zelazny

3rd September

"I love writing. I love the swirl and swing of words as they tangle with human emotions."

James Michener

4th September

"I loathe writing. On the other hand I'm a great believer in money."

S.J. Perelman

5th September

"Every novel is an attempt to capture time, to weave something solid out of air. The author knows it is an impossible task - that is why he keeps on trying."

David Beaty

6th September

"Writing is an exploration. You start from nothing and learn as you go."

E.L. Doctorow

7th September

"There are no dull subjects. There are
only dull writers."

H.L. Mencken

8th September

"Whenever you feel an impulse to perpetrate a piece of exceptionally fine writing, obey it... and delete it before sending your manuscript to the press."

Sir Arthur Quiller-Couch

9th September

"A good title should be like a good metaphor. It should intrigue without being too baffling or too obvious."

Walker Percy

10th September

"This writing business. Pencils and whatnot. Overrated, if you ask me."

Winnie the Pooh

11th September

"Have something to say, and say it as clearly as you can. That is the only secret of style."

Matthew Arnold

12th September

"The title to a work of writing is like a house's
front porch....
It should invite you to come on in."

Angela Giles Klocke

13th September

"The only certainty about writing and trying to
be a writer is that it has to be done, not dreamed
of or planned and never written, or talked about
(the ego eventually falls apart like a soaked
sponge), but simply written; it's a dreadful,
awful fact that writing is like any
other work."

Janet Frame

14th September

"Unprovided with original learning, unformed in the habits of thinking, unskilled in the art of composition, I resolved to write a book."

Edward Gibbon

15th September

"In conversation you can use timing, a look, an inflection. But on the page all you have is commas, dashes, the amount of syllables in a word. When I write, I read everything out loud to get the right rhythm."

Fran Lebowitz

16th September

"Writing is a socially acceptable form of schizophrenia."

E.L. Doctorow

17th September

"Technique alone is never enough. You have to
have passion. Technique alone is just an
embroidered potholder."

Raymond Chandler

18th September

"A writer's voice is not character alone, it is not style alone; it is far more. A writer's voice like the stroke of an artist's brush - is the thumbprint of her whole person - her idea, wit, humor, passions, rhythms."

Patricia Lee Gauch

19th September

"Many people hear voices when no one is there. Some of them are called mad and are shut up in rooms where they stare at the walls all day. Others are called writers and they do pretty much the same thing."

Meg Chittenden

20th September

"Inspiration is the act of drawing up a chair to the writing desk."

Anon

21st September

"If you tell me, it's an essay. If you show me, it's a story."

Barbara Greene

22nd September

"I always write about my own experiences,
whether I've had them or not."

Ron Carlson

23rd September

"To finish is a sadness to a writer -- a little death. He puts the last word down and it is done. But it isn't really done. The story goes on and leaves the writer behind, for no story is ever done."

John Steinbeck

24th September

"Don't tell me the moon is shining; show me the glint of light on broken glass."

Anton Chekhov

25th September

"Writing became such a process of discovery that I couldn't wait to get to work in the morning: I wanted to know what I was going to say."

Sharon O'Brien

26th September

"The most original authors are not so because they advance what is new, but because they put what they have to say as if it had never been said before."

Goethe

27th September

"A good style should show no sign of effort.
What is written should seem like a
happy accident."

W. Somerset Maugham

28th September

"With sixty staring me in the face, I have developed inflammation of the sentence structure and a definite hardening of the paragraphs."

James Thurber

29th September

"I get a lot of letters from people. They say
'I want to be a writer. What should I do?'
I tell them to stop writing to me and to get
on with it."

Ruth Rendell

30th September

"Usually, when people get to the end of a chapter, they close the book and go to sleep. I deliberately write a book so when the reader gets to the end of the chapter, he or she must turn one more page. When people tell me I've kept them up all night, I feel like I've succeeded."

Sidney Sheldon

1st October

"You have to protect your writing time.
You have to protect it to the death."

William Goldman

2nd October

"Some books are to be tasted, others to be
swallowed, and others to be chewed
and digested."

Francis Bacon

3rd October

"As cows need milking and sweet peas need picking, so writers must continually exercise their mental muscles by a daily stint."

Joan Aiken

4th October

"Like stones, words are laborious and unforgiving, and the fitting of them together, like the fitting of stones, demands great patience and strength of purpose and particular skill."

Edmund Morrison

5th October

"I learned to write by listening to people talk. I still feel that the best of my writing comes from having heard rather than having read."

Gayl Jones

6th October

"Really, in the end, the only thing that can make you a writer is the person that you are, the intensity of your feeling, the honesty of your vision, the unsentimental acknowledgment of the endless interest of the life around and within you. Virtually nobody can help you deliberately - many people will help you unintentionally."

Santha Rama Rau

7th October

"A writer's job is to imagine everything so
personally that the fiction is as vivid
as memories."

John Irving

8th October

"Employ your time in improving yourself by other men's writings so that you shall come easily by what others have labored hard for."

Socrates

9th October

"I have rewritten - often several times - every word I have ever written. My pencils outlast their erasers."

Vladimir Nabokov

10th October

"You learn by writing short stories. Keep writing
short stories. The money's in novels, but
writing short stories keeps your
writing lean and pointed."

Larry Niven

11th October

"The most valuable of talents is never using two
words when one will do."

Thomas Jefferson

12th October

"I never had any doubts about my abilities. I knew I could write. I just had to figure out how to eat while doing this."

Cormac McCarthy

13th October

"I went for years not finishing anything. Because, of course, when you finish something you can be judged. I had poems which were re-written so many times I suspect it was just a way of avoiding sending them out."

Erica Jong

14ᵗʰ October

"Success is a finished book, a stack of pages
each of which is filled with words. If you reach
that point, you have won a victory over yourself
no less impressive than sailing single-handed
around the world."

Tom Clancy

15th October

"To be a writer is to throw away a great deal, not to be satisfied, to type again, and then again and once more, and over and over."

John Hersey

16th October

"I admire anybody who has the guts to write anything at all."

E.B. White

17th October

"My most important piece of advice to all you would-be writers: when you write, try to leave out all the parts readers skip."

Elmore Leonard

18th October

"I often have to write a hundred pages or more before there's a paragraph that's alive."

Philip Roth

19th October

"You will have to write and put away or burn a lot of material before you are comfortable in this medium. You might as well start now and get the work done. For I believe that eventually quantity will make for quality."

Ray Bradbury

20th October

"Forget all the rules. Forget about being
published. Write for yourself and
celebrate writing."

Melinda Haynes

21st October

"Literature is like any other trade; you will never sell anything unless you go to the right shop."

George Bernard Shaw

22nd October

"When we read, we start at the beginning and continue until we reach the end. When we write, we start in the middle and fight our way out."

Vickie Karp

23rd October

"Talent is helpful in writing, but guts are absolutely essential."

Jessamyn West

24th October

"One writes to make a home for oneself, on paper, in time, in others' minds."

Alfred Kazin

25th October

"Success comes to a writer, as a rule, so gradually that it is always something of a shock to him to look back and realize the heights to which he has climbed."

P.G. Wodehouse

26th October

"The best way to have a good idea is to have lots of ideas."

Linus Pauling

27th October

"If you are a genius, you'll make your own rules,
but if not - and the odds are against it - go to
your desk, no matter what your mood, face the
icy challenge of the paper - write."

J.B. Priestly

28th October

"The faster I write the better my output. If I'm going slow I'm in trouble. It means I'm pushing the words instead of being pulled by them."

Raymond Chandler

29th October

"Fiction writing is great.
You can make up almost anything."

Ivana Trump

30th October

"Words are sacred. They deserve respect. If you get the right ones, in the right order, you can nudge the world a little."

Tom Stoppard

31st October

"Poetry is a deal of joy and pain and wonder,
with a dash of the dictionary."

Kahlil Gibran

1st November

"At night, when the objective world has slunk back into its cavern and left dreamers to their own, there come inspirations and capabilities impossible at any less magical and quiet hour. No one knows whether or not he is a writer unless he has tried writing at night."

H.P. Lovecraft

2nd November

"And it does no harm to repeat, as often as you can, 'Without me the literary industry would not exist: the publishers, the agents, the sub-agents, the sub-sub-agents, the accountants, the libel lawyers, the departments of literature, the professors, the theses, the books of criticism, the reviewers, the book pages - all this vast and proliferating edifice is because of this small, patronized, put-down and underpaid person.'"

Doris Lessing

3rd November

"No one is asking, let alone demanding, that you write. The world is not waiting with bated breath for your article or book. Whether or not you get a single word on paper, the sun will rise, the earth will spin, the universe will expand. Writing is forever and always a choice - your choice."

Beth Mende Conny

4th November

"The best time for planning a book is when you're doing the dishes."

Agatha Christie

5th November

"It's an adrenaline surge rushing through your body. You have this spark of an idea that keeps threatening to burst into flames and you have to get the words out on paper to match this emotion or picture in your head.
After this comes the work of cleaning up the mess that you made."

Janet West

6th November

"I put a piece of paper under my pillow, and when I could not sleep I wrote in the dark."

H.D. Thoreau

7th November

"I love deadlines. I like the whooshing sound
they make as they fly by."

Douglas Adams

8th November

"Moving around is good for creativity: the next line of dialogue that you desperately need may well be waiting in the back of the refrigerator or half a mile along your favorite walk."

Will Shetterly

9th November

"Rejection slips, or form letters, however tactfully phrased, are lacerations of the soul, if not quite inventions of the devil - but there is no way around them."

Isaac Asimov

10th November

"As I look back on what I have written,
I can see that the very persons who have taken
away my time are those who have given me
something to say."

Katherine Paterson

11th November

"In science there is a dictum: don't add an experiment to an experiment. Don't make things unnecessarily complicated. In writing fiction, the more fantastic the tale, the plainer the prose should be. Don't ask your readers to admire your words when you want them to believe your story."

Ben Bova

12th November

"Plot springs from character...
I've always sort of believed that these people
inside me - these characters - know who they
are and what they're about and what happens,
and they need me to help get it down on paper
because they don't type."

Anne Lamott

13th November

"Any man who keeps working is not a failure. He may not be a great writer, but if he applies the old-fashioned virtues of hard, constant labor, he'll eventually make some kind of career for himself as a writer."

Ray Bradbury

14th November

"Find out what your hero or heroine wants, and
when he or she wakes up in the morning,
just follow him or her all day."

Ray Bradbury

15th November

"Beware of self-indulgence. The romance
surrounding the writing profession carries
several myths: that one must suffer in order to
be creative; that one must be cantankerous and
objectionable in order to be bright; that ego is
paramount over skill; that one can rise to a level
from which one can tell the reader to go to hell.
These myths, if believed, can ruin you.
If you believe you can make a living as a writer,
you already have enough ego."

David Brin

16th November

"Don't say the old lady screamed - bring her on
and let her scream."

Mark Twain

17th November

"I have been successful probably because I have always realized that I knew nothing about writing and have merely tried to tell an interesting story entertainingly."

Edgar Rice Burroughs

18th November

"A writer should create living people; people, not characters. A character is a caricature."

Ernest Hemingway

19th November

"If you write one story, it may be bad; if you write a hundred, you have the odds in your favor."

Edgar Rice Burroughs

20th November

"When characters are really alive, before their author, the latter does nothing but follow them in their action."

Luigi Pirandello

21st November

"The reason 99% of all stories written are not bought by editors is very simple. Editors never buy manuscripts that are left on the closet shelf at home."

John Campbell

22ⁿᵈ November

"The last thing one settles in writing a book is what one should put in first."

Pascal

23rd November

"I firmly believe every book was meant
to be written."

Marchette Chute

24th November

"I rewrote the ending of 'Farewell to Arms' 39 times before I was satisfied."

Ernest Hemingway

25th November

"In writing a series of stories about the same characters, plan the whole series in advance in some detail, to avoid contradictions and inconsistencies."

L. Sprague de Camp

26th November

"If I didn't know the ending of a story, I wouldn't begin. I always write my last line, my last paragraph, my last page first."

Katherine Anne Porter

27th November

"Make everybody fall out of the plane first, and then explain who they were and why they were in the plane to begin with."

Nancy Ann Dibble

28th November

"Your characters change you. In coming to know them, you come to know an unacknowledged part of yourself. In working out their destinies in the pages of your writing, your characters work out something within you, too."

Susan Shaughnessy

29th November

"To write good SF today...
you must push further and harder, reach deeper
into your own mind until you break through into
the strange and terrible country wherein live
your own dreams."

Gardner Dozois

30th November

"Writing is rewriting... If you fall in love with the vision you want of your work and not your words, the rewriting will become easier."

Nora DeLoach

1st December

"If you start with a bang,
you won't end with a whimper."

T.S. Eliot

2nd December

"Read a ton of books before you presume to write your own. Live an interesting life. Write and prepare to be rejected."

Larry Baker

3rd December

"People on the outside think there's something magical about writing, that you go up in the attic at midnight and cast the bones and come down in the morning with a story, but it isn't like that. You sit in back of the typewriter and you work, and that's all there is to it."

Harlan Ellison

4th December

"Good characters the reader cares about
combined with an intriguing plot.
Do those two and you've got it made."

Bob Mayer

5th December

"Thank your readers and the critics who praise you, and then ignore them. Write for the most intelligent, wittiest, wisest audience in the universe: write to please yourself."

Harlan Ellison

6th December

"You have to want to write and like to write.
Sit down at that desk or machine or laptop and
tell stories."

Linda Fairstein

7th December

"It begins with a character, usually, and once he stands up on his feet and begins to move, all I can do is trot along behind him with paper and pencil trying to keep up long enough to put down what he says and does."

William Faulkner

8th December

"I only write when I am inspired. Fortunately I am inspired at 9 o'clock every morning."

William Faulkner

9th December

"Find the key emotion; this may be all you need
know to find your short story."

F. Scott Fitzgerald

10th December

"A story isn't about a moment in time, a story is about the moment in time."

W.D. Wetherell

11th December

"The greatest rules of dramatic writing are conflict, conflict, conflict."

James Frey

12th December

"I get a fine warm feeling when I'm doing well, but that pleasure is pretty much negated by the pain of getting started each day. Let's face it, writing is hell."

William Styron

13th December

"In nearly all good fiction, the basic - all but inescapable - plot form is this: A central character wants something, goes after it despite opposition (perhaps including his own doubts), and so arrives at a win, lose, or draw."

John Gardner

14th December

"In books I have traveled, not only to other worlds, but into my own. I learned who I was and who I wanted to be, what I might aspire to, and what I might dare to dream about my world and myself."

Anna Quindlen

15th December

"If you haven't got an idea, start a story anyway.
You can always throw it away, and maybe by the
time you get to the fourth page you will have an
idea, and you'll only have to throw away the
first three pages."

William Campbell Gault

16th December

"These are not books, lumps of lifeless paper,
but minds alive on the shelves."

Gilbert Highet

17th December

"In brief, I spend half my time trying to learn the secrets of other writers - to apply them to the expression of my own thoughts."

Shirley Ann Grau

18th December

"The real purpose of books is to trap the mind into doing its own thinking."

Christopher Morley

19th December

"It's none of their business that you have to learn to write. Let them think you were born that way."

Ernest Hemingway

20th December

"A great book should leave you with many experiences and slightly exhausted at the end. You live several lives while reading it."

William Styron

21st December

"A writer never has a vacation.
For a writer's life consists of either writing or
thinking about writing."

Eugene Ionesco

22nd December

"The only important thing in a book is the meaning it has for you."

W. Somerset Maugham

23rd December

"I get up in the morning, torture a typewriter
until it screams, then stop."

Clarence Budington Kelland

24th December

"I don't want to just mess with your head. I want to mess with your life... I want you to miss appointments, burn dinner, skip your homework. I want you to tell your wife to take that moonlight stroll on the beach at Waikiki with the resort tennis pro while you read a few more chapters."

Stephen King

25th December

"You may be able to take a break from writing, but you won't be able to take a break from being a writer…"

Stephen Leigh

26th December

"For several days after my first book was published, I carried it about in my pocket and took surreptitious peeps at it to make sure the ink had not faded."

Sir James M. Barrie

27th December

"Tell the readers a story. Because without a story, you are merely using words to prove you can string them together in logical sentences."

Anne McCaffrey

28th December

"I never want to see anyone, and I never want to
go anywhere or do anything.
I just want to write."

P.G. Wodehouse

29th December

"Exercise the writing muscle every day, even if it is only a letter, notes, a title list, a character sketch, a journal entry. Writers are like dancers, like athletes. Without that exercise, the muscles seize up."

Jane Yolen

30th December

"Writers write about what obsesses them. You draw those cards. I lost my mother when I was 14. My daughter died at the age of 6. I lost my faith as a Catholic. When I'm writing, the darkness is always there. I go where the pain is."

Anne Rice

31st December

"Engrave this in your brain:
EVERY WRITER GETS REJECTED.
You will be no different."

John Scalzi

Printed in the United Kingdom
by Lightning Source UK Ltd.
119939UK00001B/1